CLAY

CLAY

MANDY COE

*all the very
best

Mandy Coe.*

Shoestring Press

Typeset and printed by Q3 Print Project Management Ltd,
Loughborough, Leics
(01509) 213456

Published by Shoestring Press
19 Devonshire Avenue, Beeston, Nottingham, NG9 1BS
(0115) 925 1827
www.shoestringpress.co.uk

First published 2009
© Copyright: Mandy Coe
The moral right of the author has been asserted.
ISBN: 987 1 904886 92 1

ACKNOWLEDGEMENTS

Acknowledgements and thanks are due to editors of the following publications where some of these poems first appeared: *Acumen, Barnet Open Poetry Competition Anthology, Dream Catcher, Frogmore Papers, Magma, Rain Dog, Rialto, Yorkshire Open Poetry Competition anthology.*

The following poems were awarded first prize: *Salt, All rise* and *Mosaics;* Manchester Poetry Competition. *When we found flowers could speak;* Southport Open Poetry Competition. *Life is Simple;* the Ted Walters Memorial Prize. *Sometimes it occurs to me that I am dead;* Ilkley Festival Poetry Prize.

The writing of this book has been greatly assisted by a grant from Arts Council England.

My thanks to the Hawthornden Trust for awarding me a fellowship, giving me time to write and a chance to meet five wonderful fellows.

*"You are a little grey-black horse of clay, a kiss
of black mud, my love..." Pablo Neruda*

For Ellen and Alan White

CONTENTS

MELODY'S LAMENT

As he turns over, breathes,
I creep in
through the cracks
of a curving dream. *Will you*

forgot all of me but my echo
which he caught as his wife
clicked on the bathroom light
and he saw me
in the pattern of the blinds. *Will you*

take this
tune and make this
(hey laaa hmmmn)
joy in throat and bones.

Violin that afternoon,
practising. Fingertips light,
an ear, soft as lips.
Draw me
up from darkness, haul me,
thrashing and full into the air. *Take*
this
tune and make this

The bow exhales
a puff of resin; his elbow
shoves me aside for scales.
Hey laaa
He closes his eyes and almost
but the lark,
that bloody lark ascends.

1

MOSAICS, PIAZZA ARMERINA
Assassination of Maximilianus Hercules

For these stories to work
you must stand back, but I am pulling you close.
Your face might be pressed to the tiles,
your son-in-law's knife between your ribs,
seeing nothing but abstraction,
perhaps the swirl encircling Arione's breast.

You walked her skin a thousand times,
tigers lurching
in drunken lamplight, snaking tesserae
making the spotted hare jump,
waves shimmer beneath Hercules's ship.

You dropped a cloak in the lemon tree,
a shoe in the Queen of Sheba's lap.
You even laid a girl
among the bulls, then laughed
at the patterns on her back

The sparkle in Arione's eye
is one white square. Your blood
runs along the grout. Hesitating
at every junction, it moves
through the maze one tile at a time.

BIRTH OF THE FOSSILS

A gecko pauses, receiving.
Birds darken the sky
as petrified forests nudge bedrock.
Frenzied ants
begin to unblock a million tunnels
launching soldiers before it is too late.

In great halls, floors and pillars ripple,
exhaling clouds of sandstone dust.
Cathedral bells hum and a marble
Madonna shudders, skin crazed.

On a granite worktop a glass of wine
slides sideways. At the dinner table
a woman touches her collarbone, where,
on a silver chain,
a fly vibrates in a bubble of amber.

On the beach belemnite ink
bleeds down white cliffs
and pebbles crack like bullets.

HEAVEN

The sun stripped in seconds,
its bones fragile as glass.
I touched one, left a fingerprint.

The moon had to be wooed.
There was music, a slow dance,
fumbling with buttons and elastic.

The earth was tougher. Shy.
I had to make a lot of promises.
What do I want?

It's the reveal.
Imagination is not enough.
What happens afterwards?

Nothing. These whores
will do anything in the end.
By the time you look up

they are wrapped again
and spinning
as if nothing ever happened.

ANTS IN ZERO GRAVITY

Nothing we saw upset us.
We knew planets and blackness.
We knew blackness like no one else.
Between two sheets of glass
we tunnelled and touched as we had at home.
We were even given names.

It wasn't nebula radiation, or upside-down faces
floating past with clipboards.
It wasn't g-forces
that gave us such acid terror. Even the explosion;
the fireball. None of that scared us.
It was the tree,
the tree roots cracking the base of our anthill.
One more rainy season...

Our particles circle the earth now.
We try to keep close,
but solar winds do their job.
The blue earth flashes us glimpses
of continents wreathed in cloud.

SOMETIMES IT OCCURS TO ME THAT I AM DEAD

No, stop and stay are meaningless.
Clothes are not quick enough. It is ridiculous
how I long for the rough wool collar of a coat,
the tight brim of a hat, the cold grip of shoes.

I was clumsy when I started; a woman shrieked,
dropped a plate, a man dropped to his knees.
I hate the gritty suck of concrete, but have grown
to love the slow swim of glass. If I am tempted

by floors I'll be done for. I try to remember
what falling meant: the explosion of breath,
a splintering of bone, the hammer of earth
swinging up. If I lean forward and close my eyes

the world spins, passing through me
like indigestion. A tree x-rays my lungs,
a blackbird sings as it slides through my ribs.

CREATIONIST HOMEWORK

Making a child took a billion years
(seven minutes of soft cries, decades of indigestion:
onions, palm hearts, ginger;
centuries of labour).

Now a moon is stapled to sky,
horizons are pinking-sheared
and three clouds sellotaped in a line.

I sprinkle silver-dust onto invisible words,
blobs of glue shaped like the Galapagos.
Tilting the sheet of sugar-paper
reveals *shalom, greetings, salaam*.
Rolling it up, I snap on a red elastic band;
my child goes to school trailing glitter.

SUNFLOWER SEX

is loud. Here they are!
Barely dressed in tiny frills
as hollow stalks thrust them
whooping into the sky.

Van Gogh heard it,
saw how fast yellow bunting
shrivels and falls.
Quick!

A black and white army
of seed must ripen here.
Birds hop along fences
sharpening their beaks.

DRAW

A man gave me this dog.
Because he drew her she's only got two legs,
but from the side she looks just fine.

I won her in a game of dice: an eight throw.
She's got an alligator grin
that keeps away kids and thugs.

Go ahead, she won't bite,
she only looks that way
because the guy drew her at night

when he was rat-arsed drunk.
I heard he drew a man a house: an IOU
on the two fifteen. It had a garden with a tree,

but it belonged to Stelkie Murray
and you don't draw what isn't yours.
There are rules.

I tried it once – licked the lead,
drew a coin. Tried to spend it
but it was dud.

Guess I don't have an eye for art
but next time I play Leonardo
I'll sleeve an ace;

make him draw me a girl,
and if he's not too drunk,
I'll get him to draw her from the front.

OUTRAGEOUS GIANTS

Sancho laughs and points,
dancing from foot to foot
while his donkey soft-lips the weeds
round a car-park bollard.

Pressing his hands
to the small of his back,
Sancho laughs so hard
his hat falls off.

Slapping his thighs he bends forward
shoulders shaking.
The donkey looks up,
still chewing.

A boy with wrecked skin
and narrow shoulder blades
shunts a conga of shopping trolleys.
Sanchez closes his eyes and howls.

A woman thunks down the boot of her Volvo,
wipes her palms and comes over;
Excuse me, she says,
I wonder if you could move your donkey.

WHEN MARY TOFTS GAVE BIRTH TO RABBITS
Hogarth (1726)

The midwife lifted her eyes,
then raised her bloodied hands, cupped
and offering me the chance
to cry out or fall in love
as fathers do.

I am a Waterloo sweep
who knows how to lay out sheets;
the weight of brushes and rods.
I've seen tumbling rooks
clap up a storm of soot.

But my stare makes no sense of this:
no crumpled face,
no fists, no kicking feet.
This baby is in six parts,
each stirring, each one blind.

The midwife fills her lap
and with an apron corner
begins to rub
squirming scraps of fur.
She nods to the other three.

There are many things a father can do
when faced with this.
I can think of none
and tugging out a shirt tail,
begin to smooth a tiny head, back, ears.

11

PAID

diolch, nkosi, shur-nur-ah-gah-lem
    men's profiles, dates,
    thumbnail the ridged never-ending
    this one spinning – a sun of gold
    smacked into stillness

danke, merci, gracias
    buffalo, wren, a ship full of cotton
    riding tiny waves
    wet bar, slap, slide, men with visors
    heaving bags into armoured vans

dhanyabad, blagodaria, hvala
    raining from a blinding sky
    missed one! missed one!
    sharp-boned children spider
    in the dust of a roaring jeep

shukran gazillan, yakoke, nandi
    two, four, six, eight:
    maize, milk, rent
    bite it, sew it into your hem
    hurry through the dark

mh goi, abarka, mille grazie
    a silver-mouthed fountain
    spews a river of noise
    a woman screams again and again
    a plastic tub overflows

dziekuje, bhala hove, shakkran
    an uncle walks
    ten minutes of his day
    across the back of calloused fingers
    pulls five warm minutes from your ear

12

LIFE IS SIMPLE

Words are often chalked on the underside of tables.
Bare feet are humble.
The horn of a goat is warm.
In flour-bins live tiny beetles.
Licking allows you to get to know a person really well.
If we were slower beasts than we are
stars would appear as brilliant rings
– ripples from a stone.

Cats eat grass then vomit onto books.
Breathing burns calories.
A toilet seat leaves a mark like a horse's hoof.
Elephants die when their teeth wear out.
String is always twisted clockwise.
If we were slower beasts than we are
waterfalls would flatten into a curtain of light,
clouds would vault from one horizon to the other.

Bathroom mirrors get splattered with toothpaste.
A slap leaves a handprint.
Turn-ups fill with sand even if you haven't been on a beach.
Parents die.
If we were slower beasts than we are
hair would spill from our skin.
Like fruit, we would rise and swell, shrink and fall.

SHEELIN
(faery lake)

Fish crisscross above us,
leaping for midges bullseyed in rings of silver.
We don't make curses, yet
when the deer's lips sucked greedily
at the edge of our sky (it was a dry summer
and our world had shrunk)
we did speak of her unkindly.

October rains released
her fawn's bones from the mud:
delicate skull, buds of antlers.
Silt stirs at our every move,
the farmer's daughter dances up a storm.
Her white shoulders glow as she circles
but her eyes never leave the boy.

We rock in their tides.
Near them, icy water warms.
Rising from the darkness we come closer;
stroke. She squeals, he sighs.
It is not like the violence of floods,
the slow sadness of drought.
Not like the child with the blackened eye
who hurled rock after rock. Or the drunk
kneeling to part the reeds
and plead with his own reflection.

These two are the stuff of bones:
smooth and pale. As they shudder
seed-pearl bubbles tremble on their skin.
Picking them off we taste salt, taste air.

LET'S CELEBRATE

the moments
where nothing happens.
The moments
that fill our lives.
Not the field bright with poppies, but
the times you walked, seeing
no leaves, no sky, only one foot
after another.

We are sleeping
(it's not midnight and
there is no dream).
We enter a room – no one is in it.
We run a tap,
queue to buy a stamp.

These are the straw moments
that give substance
to our astonishments;
moments the homesick dream of;
the bereaved, the diagnosed.

JUMP

When we catch the train,
run fast enough and jump,
we will see through open wagon doors
bruised plains slipping past,
red sky and mountains,
there will be no north, only
east and west and south.

When we catch the train,
your weight and my weight
will be a thing to dream of,
the give of shale, the hiss of grass,
the swing of legs, and the leap
as motion matches motion.
A shirt is hauled with both hands,
a finger-nail broken.

The citrus fruit we stole
will tumble from our pockets
and we will gasp and laugh,
our faces pressed to the rough wooden floor.

As tracks flicker between floor-slats,
a lemon rolls in and out of sun and shade,
then bounces out the open door.

SALT

He tasted me
before I boarded the ship,
picked me out from the others,
leaned forward and licked my face
with a tongue strong and pink as a calf's.
I could have left then,

shot into the sky. I could have
gone to live on the other side of the clouds,
but the jetty pressed against my bare feet,
cold stone drawing hot piss low in my belly.

The harbour echoed with shouts,
the drag of chains, the thunder of barrels rolling.
A rat squeezed out of a porthole and dropped.
Men peered at the stinking water; threw stones.

He tasted me
and I smelled meat and wine on his breath.
In that close moment I saw the pores of his skin,
the curve of an earlobe, bushy eyebrows
tangled as the ship's masts and ropes.
The wetness on my cheek cooled in the breeze.

He held out his tongue, wiped it on his sleeve,
laughing and speaking to the man with the pen,
who looked at me, wrote down a name.

KOLKATA

I   Forget or Believe

(i) In New York, Joel Grey performed
    The Threepenny Opera backwards.
    Bending his arms and legs
    in time to each tango; wearing a mask
    on the back of his head
    he made us forget – or believe.

    Legless beggars, crooked sheriff,
    Mackheath's knife, Joel Grey sang
    about them all; white face immobile.
    But I did notice his thumbs
    – on the wrong side of his hands.

(ii) Downstream of Kolkata, record high tides
     made mangrove islands rustle with hungry tigers.
     Fishermen, desperate to harvest honey,
     wore masks on the backs of their heads.
     At first the tigers faltered,
     they usually bite the back of the neck,
     but a village on the banks of the Hooghly
     has been renamed The Place of Widows.

     With bare feet the women
     spread small mounds of rice to dry on the levee.
     Raising one leg at a time they rescue
     precious grains from between their toes.
     Saris flutter in the wind, the muddy river
     reflecting an orange and turquoise dance.

II ALL GOING TO THE BAY OF BENGAL

Beneath Rabindra Setu Bridge a river slides.
And here is a smaller one, aimed
from a fisted hand, darkening dust
down the wall, joining the spill
from the chapatti vendor's bowl.

Pump water is scooped into armpits,
soap-foam rinsed from a bowed head.
A red fountain arches
from the pursed lips of a taxi driver.

Our feet dance between reeking puddles
where a dog links puppies with a delta of milk.
We are hot. So thirsty. Sugarcane-presses
squeeze a burst of sweetness onto our lips.
A machete hacks green coconut;
we dip straws into the dark.

III SMOKE

is on my lips, my tongue finds it
rough on the roof of my mouth.

Through permanent dusk
the sun is a pale moon. This is the City's edge,
where meat is steamed into leather,
molten steel hisses into shape and chimneys
tower over kilns filled with rough bricks
imprinted with the hands of men.

Beside me blue flame heats an oil barrel,
circles of dough slapped against
its blackened walls. Broken, the bread exhales
white curls of steam. I breathe in,
fragments of city swarming my lungs.

IV   GOAT ON A BICYCLE

Two boys on a rusted bike, a blur
of spokes and bare feet. The hot breeze
parts to let them pass. One stands and peddles,
rises and falls, hips against handlebars.
The other, legs straight out, whoops, *chalo, chalo!*

The white goat lies across the crossbar,
belching up the short brown grass of the Maidan.
Her pot belly is pushed up and out one side,
her head cranes round; yellow eyes wide.

From deep within her a jolted bleat
whips past us and we wince
at the spit of tyres on gravel.
Even when they are small with distance
we know they are so sharp with life
they tear away a part of ours. We are the ones,
barely seen, now gone. Whereas they,
in full colour, will ride this path home again

to a burnt tea and a mother grumbling
about the goat's thin milk,
its limping gait. And them, swearing
they *did* walk her back, no dawdling
at Eden Gardens, no Test Match
spectacular with sticks and a balled-up sock.

IN LOVE WITH A MAP

First I looked at it
then whispered its name.
It didn't take long to get naked,
ink staining elbows and thighs.

The paper tore a little along folds
weakened from all those travels.
I remember us
spreading it on the car bonnet,
air shimmering with heat.

Then, pinned flat with stones
in that field. We lay, watching insects
leap onto its surface: giants!
I could be vulgar, roll it up,
or slide along its edge. But it's not like that.

Just to open it out, press my skin
to the places we went. My nipple
eclipsing that mountain,
my lips on the sea.

BLINDFOLD

Noises become sharper,
the world tilts, whispers
in my ear like a drunk.

It brings the skin of my face alive
– a strip of torn shirt?
A scarf? The knot is off-centre.

I would like to raise my hands,
confirm its weave.
Where it presses my eyelids

psychedelic flowers bloom.
Of course there is more:
a hand in my back, a car door,

the gentle press of acceleration.
But that is out there
and I am here, bound

with darkness and breathing
through my mouth so as not to miss
the one sound that could save me.

ILLEGAL

I crawl through dust
where gullies turn their backs on the sea;
a man comes to me

in a fast, straight line as if I am
the answer to a question.

I hold my shadow underneath;
a dark flattened child.
When he touches me
with the side of his boot
he doesn't ask.

ZAPATAS PARK, MEXICO CITY

In silver eucalyptus light
elderly men and women move in rows.
The music falters and someone
winds a brass key – one two three
– a rhythmic clockwork sound.

The cherry-wood music box
glows in the sunlight
as beneath its small cracked window
a silver-toothed barrel rolls.
I walk over and a man points to my eyes,
his feet. I watch, trying

to follow his polished shoes
stepping through leaf-shaped patches
of sun and shade. I smile, he smiles.
Along the row, men and women
lean forward, look at me; we all smile.

Then, suddenly I am alone;
as every man turns to a partner,
spinning them into salsa.
I sit on a wall, warm with afternoon heat.
No one has spoken.

VEGETABLE LAMB
Planta Tartarica Barometz

Tiny buds of white, light as thistledown.
You must pick them before they fall.
There is no blood or bone, only wool
finer than any seen before. I promise
you madam, when woven, this cloth
can take up any colour.

We have never seen the infants born
– forgive me madam but there is no labour,
no mutton to mother and suckle – only
leaf and twig and root. It is as if the core
of the lamb has not yet grown into its coat.
It is said the plants bend at the stem, then
drop the young who trot into the night,
birth-stalk still attached.

I have ordered cuttings
and young plants taken. Picture it
madam, your lord's fields
bursting with this tranquil flock.
No need for slaughter, no need
for men to herd and shear,
no fear of the wolf.

LISTENING TO FLIES

In the gleeful prediction of a fly
this eye will shrivel, the blue of it will glaze.
Flies tell themselves these things
observing the world,
sending prophecies humming into the air.
This eye, they say,
this eye, those lips, that apple, this weak sow.

I own this blue eye and I own the sow.
As I brush flies from her face she grunts,
swollen sides heaving.
I bite into the apple, drop half into the pen.

My sow tells me about her labour,
one sound at a time.
She is full of piglets. Three are hard and still.

Last night I lay in the field
and heard the worms.
What do they say? asks my girl.
What kind of liar am I? Good enough
not to tell her! She would squeal.
She would leap up from the grass
pulling down her skirt,
How awful, she would say, *how could you
make up these things?*

So I don't tell her
the prayers of worms.
What the flies say about her lips,
about the three blue bodies
I will pull free tomorrow.

CLOCK MENDER

Clocks want to die, all of them
working out their final breath.
But I continue to resuscitate,
demanding obedience.
I have felt the resistance of the winding key;
know full well the sharp-toothed ratchet
that stops a spring from spending itself
with the whip of a snake.

I enter their hearts through secret doors,
oystering open watches to tease
order from their core.
My magnified eye follows tweezers
fine as fishbones. The whorls of my fingertips
sparkle with salt. I see the jewelled geometry
of wheels and cogs, pin-head screws;
watch-hands, small as beetle limbs.

The room is filled with ticking.
Brass pendulums cut through air,
lead weights descend on cat-gut twine.
An enamelled moon arcs
behind the sins of Adam and Eve.
A wooden bird pantomimes Spring.

FIELD OF CROWS

My eye is level with the grass.
Crows have such big thighs!
They walk about; one jumps a little.

This field was due to take off:
a tatty green carpet.
The crows, evenly spaced, hold it down;
delivering stabbing thrusts as if to teach it a lesson.
Sometimes they all look up
at the same time checking the tilt of horizon.

This field has crows in it.
And a woman
flat on her back.
Subtly the crows redistribute,
factoring in her added weight.

THE BREATH OF ROCKS

Blackdamp pools at your feet
in puddles that leave boots dry.
Scratching your head, thinking only about supper
or the curve of a woman's breast,
you are already waist high in its rising tide.

Whitedamp, the light-fingered thief,
works the post-explosion crowd, slipping in
under the dizzy guise of shock.
Touching your hot brow to the cool seam
thanking God for your life,
your lungs are already filling with shine.

Stinkdamp. Time flattened a continent,
the way a son might straight-arm a pillow
onto the face of a dying man.
This secret cannot be shared
only stumbled upon. You turn away,
the back of your hand rubbing at your lips.
No spit can rid you of its taste.

Firedamp roosts in the shadows of ceilings.
Raise your lamp
and above ground, your mother
will notice her tea dancing with ripples,
the mid-afternoon silence broken
by shouts and the sound of people running.

WHY I JUMPED

She calls to me while I sleep.
Some nights she takes
the shape of my left horn.
I saw her once, reflected
in the eye of the calf they took.
She does not flick me with a stick.
She fills puddles with milk.
She brushes my coat with silver.
I have been saying her name since I was born.

How did I do it?
I sent down a thought to each muddy leg:
we no longer belong to this meadow.

VANISHING POINT

You know how glass
can reflect sunlight? How,
from the other side of a valley, a window
will flash bright as a warning flare.

Well this didn't happen.
Neither did he see the van,
the two men, suckers in their hands,
grunting as they shuffled

a vast square of nothing across the road.
Afterwards he spoke of angles, reflections.
Suddenly seeing both ahead
and behind: bike meeting bike;

himself meeting himself.
We swapped, he laughs,
touching the scar on his forehead.
I used to be the one without this.

32

SPILL

There was no table cloth as white
as the precious Irish linen you saved
for the special event that never came.
I smooth it out on the kitchen table,
sharp fold-creases
forming a raised cross
among plates and glasses.

But laying out a spill of silver cutlery
I knock over a bottle of wine
only to see it roll and spill
and *fuck, fuck, fuck*
the choice

of mopping a little
then greeting mourners or
tearing it off
in a torrent of broken plates and glasses,
running with it in my arms
to the sink
to scrub and rinse the stain away,
make it white again.

VIELLE Á ROUE

Small black hands are buried
in Septo's silver hair,
and where feet dance and grip
his overcoat shoulder shines with grease.
The monkey brings in extra, he says,
but according to Septo's wife – only fleas.

Each night she attacks the spill of change,
lips moving, one finger sliding it,
coin by coin, into the tin.
Two wrinkled faces watch her
turn from table to cooker and back again,
banging down three plates,
three cups, three spoons.

But when winter gnaws at her bones
and Mrs Septo slumps, half dressed and helpless,
the monkey laces her boots;
fingers and teeth tugging at leather.

For a moment
she cradles its head, feels the inhuman heat,
and as its deep brown eyes meet hers,
birds drop scarlet feathers
and shimmering columns of light
descend from cathedral trees.

Septo's snoring
fills the room with the stink of breath,
grey clouds skim chimney pots.
As Mrs Septo rocks,
the monkey plays a silent tune
on the buttons of her blouse.

FATHER IN HEAVEN

In the chapel doorway
the bride is a silhouette, behind her
a dazzling plain. To the east the twister
drags its own portion of black sky.

Mrs Macready presses out
the broken chord that summons the storm,
the wet-dog breath of it
stirs the bride's veil
with the hot smell of dust and hair-oil.

For too long the decision teeters
on the height of bridesmaids' heels,
the perilous billows of polyester,
the elderly priest and length of the aisle.
This is how I was born

fatherless in this town,
unsaid vows and a groom
who, at the storm-cellar door,
didn't stop running. Twister took him
mother says as we sit on the porch.

We watch the sky for messages;
cloud-shaped stories and migrating birds
who know my father
would have called me William.

EX VOTO
tempera on wood, 1576, Barcelona Maritime Museum

The sky is purple, the mast broken.
Hands rise like lilies from black water.
The torn sail hangs
and the dead, arms crossed,
lean against walls of water
to watch the show.

Lightning pins down the horizon
as in a yellow mist,
Christopher de Villa Nova appears,
hand raised in a blessing,
white robe dry and still.

Tonight he is here for Sebastian Gara,
plucking him from roaring water
to be dropped on all fours
into the stink of a seaweed beach.

He is here to untangle Manuel Alaio
from rope and canvas, drape him
on a barnacled rock, to be rescued
by fishermen at dawn.

Nameless men cry out and pray,
the ship topples – its hull a whale,
the saints' names taste of salt.

DAY

I was born (no pain)
and was young
for the longest time. Pink
and baby blue. Lots of singing
and washing and patting dry of skin.
So many things to happen.
A game of chase, new words
learned, another language became extinct.
There was a war. A mother wept.
It rained. People looked
at their watches. Then they ate.
Someone ironed a shirt. Rabbits ran,
teenagers kissed leaning against a schoolyard wall.
A book was finished, another dropped into a bath.
Someone went to court, someone
cemented the last roof tile on a new house.
A really old panda died in a zoo.
Confetti was thrown; a river burst its banks.
People ate again.
Millions watched a rocket launched into space.
Somebody yawned.
A star came out.
There was greyness, blueness.
A girl smeared on pink lipstick.
It was time.
People closed their eyes, folded their hands.

WHEN WE FOUND FLOWERS COULD SPEAK

people grieved
for all the blooms they'd cut.
Others argued that speech
didn't necessarily mean a soul and so we learned
to avoid the most vocal:
chrysanthemums, geraniums.
Who wanted them
in their cut-glass gatherings
howling for bees and sky?

Weddings were ruined by keening bouquets,
the cat-calls of button-hole carnations.
Hearses drove slowly past,
trailing a clamour of wreaths.
A few refused to mow their lawns
because of daises. A family
was struck by a car as they crouched
listening to ragwort on the hard shoulder.
A man was arrested in the park
rubbing fistfuls of roses onto his bare skin
just to hear them cry.

KISS

The bee would have been easier dead,
but on impulse I caught one in a rose.
Its stinging parts pressed into the stamens,
transparent wings buzzing against my lips.
Afterwards I found pollen on my chin.
All I remember is perfume and fear;
petals angrily humming.

The rainbow drew me to the puddle.
On my knees, my arse rose like the tower of Pisa,
shoppers walked round me muttering about religion.
I should not have done it from the kerb.
My trembling arms could not hold my weight
and I toppled forward. My knees hurt for days.

Ice was wonderful. I did it three times.
A sharp pain at first, then a dull ache.
It left my lips stinging and wet: the power
of my kiss melting its surface. Through this
triangle snapped from the edge of a pond
the world was sheened in silver.

Sand kissed me! A damp layer lifted
to leave a tiny pale mouth on the beach.
I spat, scrubbed my mouth with a sleeve.

The bedroom ceiling – wish I hadn't.
Wrestling with the step-ladder, tilting my head
as if my neck was broken,
I had no idea Artex was so sharp.
Now I lie in bed and it's all I can see:
me up that ladder, looking like a fool.

ALL RISE

Although she was terrible at maths,
she still has the lightning ability
to measure the speed of the organist
What a friend we have in Jesus,
and multiply this by the number of verses.
This hymn
O what peace we often forfeit,
O what needless pain we bear,
will last for years.

She sways: tiny arcs of grief.
Have we trials and temptations?
Is there trouble anywhere?
Behind her, that woman:
sweet voiced. Whereas she
struggles, trapped in a key
Are we weak and heavy laden,
cumbered with a load of care?
that keeps her a child.

She could kill the bitch;
vault over pews and rip tissue-thin pages
from her book. The organist wouldn't stop
What a privilege to carry
everything to God in prayer!
but the singing would. Mourners turning
to watch the swirl of tumbling paper.
In his arms he'll take and shield thee;
thou wilt find a solace there.

LITTLE HOUSE

You were so tall.
Taller than the wardrobe,
taller than trees. I thought
the word 'dad' meant tall.

You gripped my hands
as I stood on your toes
– the only time I felt the bliss
of dancing without counting. Another time
I rode your shoulders, terrified
you would forget
and plough through a doorway.
But most of the time I ran from your voice
as it flooded rooms like a searchlight.

You made us a doll's house.
It had a battery and little lights. At night
I would crouch and peer in through the windows,
shrinking myself with play.
When you put your fist
through the doors and walls of our home,
it was as though you were trapped
the way my dolls were,
doubled up; squeezed into tiny rooms.

I would like to be a giant, go back in time.
I would pluck you out of that house.
How your family would watch, open mouthed,
as you shot up into the sky.

RINGERS

We learn by candlelight with blind bells,
clappers tied,
graveyard owls flushed from the belfry
by the whoosh of dumbed metal.
Steam rises from our heads
and we hug our arms to hide the tremble.

Girls know gripping the sally
gives us strong hands,
we can lift them by the waist over any gate.
She's a tenor, we'd say,
this one's a treble.

We follow the call: dodging and hunting,
shirts black with sweat.
Hand stroke, back stroke. Thinking,
but not thinking, like harvesting a furrow,
like dancing along a bench
when you're too drunk to walk.

These iron bells are ours,
tolling for planting, harvest home;
Passing Bell for the sick, Nine Tailors for dead.
When a mother came crying
that her lad was lost in fog we rang five hours
before he crawled from the marsh.

Cuts of light slice the belfry floor,
pigeons puff-chest in the tower.
One man takes a deep breath,
another rolls his shoulders.
The caller takes his last drag
of smoke and toes it out.
We look up and raise our hands.

ABBASSO IL TANGO
down with tango

Like a crow among scarecrows,
water in a pan of fat, I imagine peace
as something still. Lay me down

gently, I belong beneath your weight.
The liquored air is sweet as rotting plums.
We are pressed from thigh to cheek,

sweat trickles between my breasts.
Through the soles of my shoes I feel the bite
of nail-heads rising from loosened boards.

We danced this night as thin as silk.
I could puncture it with a finger, slide
through the rip. Outside the sky is dark

with the start of another year. Over the whip
of music someone starts a countdown,
by *three* we have all joined in.

ASSEMBLING

It makes me think of clowns
who twist sausage dogs from squeaking balloons.
The air is hot with the smell of plastic,
the clock, as far away as the moon.
We sit in rows, back to back,
reading each other's moods
by the hunch of shoulders, a roll of the head.

A tangle of gossip tugs us backwards,
we speak corner-mouthed
as the supervisor passes.
We make nothing,
scraps of nothing collect under our feet.
We cut, fold, build and stack.
Behind us a pen clicks
and ticks off boxes on a clipboard.

One of us is leaving but is keeping it secret.
One of us is in love
with someone they shouldn't be.
On a washroom sink an engagement ring
lies forgotten in a lather of soap bubbles.
Inside a locker door a photo of a baby
is framed with black electrical tape.
Going outside we cough
the dust of nothing into our fists.

JOHN SOANE
(Architect 1753-1837)

I want a desk, plans,
mahogany drawers with a silver key.
I want to understand arches,
weight-bearing columns.
I want to walk past a palace: *I built that,*
undress the Bank of England by running a finger
along lines I drew. I want to put in a wall-plug
strong enough to hold up a Hogarth.

Once I built a flat-pack wardrobe.
Connecting 'a' to 'b' and twisting allen keys
deep into crumbling mdf,
the wire from my underwired bra
came stabbing out.
I thought it was a heart attack.

As I lay among the screws and cardboard
I calmed myself by trying to see
shapes of countries in the ceiling cracks.
I want to take a hammer to my roof and let in light.

SING

We watch the way men wade,
making tiny waves with their thighs.
Then the decision is made and they dive.
We sit on the beach considering
the harmonics of sin.
Father fetches us ice-cream.

He will not go in the water;
won't even paddle.
When the rip-tide threatened
to spin us sisters out to sea,
he yelled for mother,

whose familiar shape
bowed deckchair stripes into one blue curve.
With her back to us, she sang us in.
Father tried to hide his trembling hands
by scrubbing us down with a sandy towel.

We sit on the sand
licking between the wafers.

IF LIGHT IS A WAVE

Light shakes out sheets
in billows, a lover's breasts and hips,
ripples of flesh on a smacked arse.

Something carries the gleam of whisky
from the glass on the bedside table,
shadows pool under the bed.

Afternoon sunshine is captured in your eye,
I see myself silhouetted, a tiny burglar,
sliding in as you blink.

Between us – aether. Here, the gloss
of lips and tongue.
We enter

a trembling bubble of soap,
swarming continents of colour.
Everything almost over.

NOT ALIVE, ALIVE, DEAD

Remember when you couldn't remember
where you were one morning, as if
your bed were standing on end, or turned about?

How the familiar looked abstract
and you considered an angle of cupboard,
a fold of curtain, and how for a moment
you were released from the grind of recall.

Remember those seconds when you nearly
fell asleep but didn't quite fall,
that delicious
slide into another realm.
Not alive... alive... dead,

there must be a little join between these states,
a moment when cells divide enough;
a woman pushes enough;
when your heart flaps like a shot bird,

once, twice, once more,
so much loss you are light with it.

YOU ONLY NOTICE STAIRS DURING STRANGE TIMES

In a comic-strip home
dad lies farting in the bath
while neighbours sip coffee
in the kitchen beneath.

Without stairs,
folding this short distance
into a long one, nothing separates
the private and public universe
but a layer of floorboards and carpet.

Stair-space is mysterious;
altering time and matter.
We shout up or down, understanding
sound-waves need that extra push
and we avoid passing on stairs,
knowing that on the molecular level
it is deeply wrong.

We sit on stairs at times of waiting or loss.
The zigzag of air above us
is too large. A space
only the bravest decorator will paint.

CENTRELESS YEAR

A hissing roar in the blackness
tells me where the ocean is.
My feet sink into sand and I walk
the treacle walk of nightmares, grasping
handfuls of dark to pull myself along.
There is a noise out there. A choking cry.

I am too young for this kind of beach,
but Dad's gone and we have no home.
This seaside mile is as unfamiliar
as anywhere else in this centreless year.

In the town above the cliffs
children sleep, skin salty from paddling,
hotel sheets tucked so tight they lie with pointed toes.
Up there pennies clatter into silver trays,
the bingo-caller is two numbers from 'House'.

Icy water burns my legs. My clothes cling
stiff as leather. I wade beyond heart-stop,
lungs closing into fists as I push out
and over the edge of the world.

In our lodgings there's a smell of gravy,
a brass gong calls guests for dinner.
Mum sits on the bed
plucking a chenille bedspread
– one strand for every month of marriage.

Reaching out I find someone
shockingly solid. I drag him... to where?
The shore is black and I am swallowing sky.
But my mind seems to hold a map of darkness
and I drag this man's misery up the beach.
He heaves up salty spumes and we grip each other.
There's no point he says, and I reply
with the only mantra a teenager knows:
It'll be alright. It'll be alright.

When I get back, Mum asks
if it has been raining. The meter has run out
and I peel wet clothes off in the dark.

I IMAGINE

you are looking out of a window
and seeing the waves on the beach or
maybe a garden with a washing line
and a blue plastic paddling pool. Perhaps
you are watching the horizon
of a big city – New York or London.

Is it quiet where you are? Can I ask you
to hear something for me?

You are listening so hard.
Your head is slightly tilted,
your eyes are unfocussed.
I hope you can hear a lovely thing:
an ice-cream van or a bird.

I haven't eaten ice-cream for years,
I remember biting off the end of the cone,
sucking it
the way you would drink sky from a tap.
When I licked my wrist my tongue was cold.

You are thinking of something else now:
it's getting dark, it's time, was that the doorbell?
You have to go. I understand.

GONE

I ask not out of sadness
but astonishment. It is as unimaginable
as water falling upward.
And hearing it over and over
makes it no less
bloody ridiculous:
gormless, golem, gnome, gone.

A trollish lack of logic spawned this word.
In death, I believe – but where? Where?

CLAY

it melts metal this heat
puddles sand
I will send my work to hell hoping
its secret bubble of fear
won't explode

spreading cool orange blood
the clay bends
my fingers to its heart
draws my palms flat
against its smooth sides
spins me
to dip in the well of its o

the weight of raw meat
smelling of rain
it is given from the earth knowing
it will be returned
gravity tugging it back to smash
curves to points
points to dust
but now

it rises up
a slippery stem of an idea pushing
through my clumsy fists